PLANNING YOUR RETIREMENT INCOME

DIANNE B. TERRY

Printed in the United States of America

Réalta Publications

First Printing, 2020

ISBN: 978-1-950591-08-4

presented in this book. It is your responsibility to conduct your own due diligence regarding the safe and successful operation of your business if you intend to apply any of our information in any way to your business operations.

Terms of Use

You are given a non-transferable, "personal use" license to this book. You cannot distribute it or share it with other individuals.

Also, there are no resale rights or private label rights granted when purchasing this book. In other words, it's for your own personal use only.

PLANNING YOUR RETIREMENT INCOME

Réalta Publications
Shawnee, Kansas

Table of Contents

Chapter 1- Introduction 1

Chapter 2 – Social Security 9
    Social Security Tax.. 9
    Full-Benefit Retirement Age 10
    Early Retirement 11
    Delayed Retirement 12
    Marriage and Social Security..................................... 12
    Divorce and Social Security 13
    Your Own Social Security Account............................. 15
    Your Social Security Work History 15

Chapter 3 – Pension Plans 17
    Survivor Benefits 18

Chapter 4 – Annuities 21
    Survivor Benefits 22
    Communication.. 23

Chapter 5 – Misc Sources 25
    Bank Accounts & CDs 25
    If Your Home is Paid Off.. 26
    What if Your home is not paid off? 29

Chapter 6 – Qualified Plans...33
    401(k).. 34
    Solo 401(k) 46
    403(b).. 47
    457 49
    What if you've worked multiple places?..................... 49
    What if you're married?.. 51

Chapter 7 – Non-Qualified and Misc Plans.......................53
    Non-Qualified Plans.. 53
    Misc Plans 54

Chapter 8 – Withdrawals 59

Chapter 9 - Calculations 66

Resource Guide 70

Author Page 74

More Books and Resources from the Author 76

Appendix A: Retirement Income Workbook...................78

Chapter 1- Introduction

You've worked all your adult life with one goal in mind . . . retirement. You're a planner: you've saved, calculated and planned out your life. You know when you're going to retire and exactly what life is going to look like. You're just waiting for that day—Day One of your new life.

On the other hand, maybe you're not really a planner. Like many Americans, retirement has always been "out there" somewhere in the future. You know it will come some day, but you haven't worried too much about it because life if just busy. You have dreamed about the perfect retirement and someday, when the time is right, things will fall into place and your retirement will be . . . epic!

Whether you are a planner or not, this book is for you. Use it as a checklist to ensure you've thought of all your potential sources of income. Finally settle that queasy feeling you have had for years about whether you can afford to retire someday.

Our Grandparents' Lifestyle

Fifty years ago, people retired knowing they would have Social Security and possibly a pension. They had survived the Great Depression—some of the darkest financial days the United States ever knew.

Our grandparents and even our parents lived more simply as a result: they saved money, paid off their mortgages, only had one car and lived within their means. They knew how to do without when times were lean and how to save money when times were good.

In many cases, they were better situated to retire than most of us will ever be. Working in the garden, spending time making things in the garage, and growing old with family surrounding them was a life they had been training for all their lives. Their generation knew how to live within their means.

Life was good.

Our Lifestyles

Fast forward fifty years to our generation. We haven't done such a great job of retaining the knowledge and lifestyle our grandparent and parents tried to pass down to us. Our paychecks have grown but so have our desires for more—more house(s), more cars, more "things". We spend as much as we make and then some.

Our work habits have changed, too. We tend to change jobs every four years or so, showing no long-term loyalty or tenure at a single company. Definitely not like our grandparents, so no gold watch at retirement on OUR horizons.

And when it comes to paying off our homes so we can be mortgage-free at retirement? That outlook is not very good, either. How many people do you know who have been in their homes all their lives or even more than twenty-five or thirty years? Over the past forty years, people moved on average every eight years—because of jobs, having children, or retiring. Recently, the average tenure has grown somewhat, but we still aren't staying in a home long enough to pay it off.

What about saving money? Well . . . we haven't done a very good job of that, either. Many people I've talked to over the past two or three years say they will have to work well past the age of 65 because they fear they won't have enough money to retire. Over half say they are concerned they won't have money to live comfortably in retirement.

So, where does that leave us? We don't have as much money saved as our grandparents and we don't have our mortgages paid off.

There's something even more impactful to our retirement finances, though. Our plans for retirement are much, much more grandiose than what Grandpa and Grandma expected.

We want to travel, stay active, maybe move to another state or country, re-invent ourselves, volunteer, go back to school, and pursue "all. the. things." we didn't make time for while we were working.

How will we pay for this dream retirement? How much planning and money will that take?

It probably won't happen on Social Security and a pension—at least not in this country. We will have to rely on our savings as well.

Communication

If you are married, you must discuss retirement together. This is one of those exercises that is going to require communication. Probably not what you want to hear, I'm sure. It's been my experience that most couples don't like to sit down and discuss finances . . . and this is going to be a long discussion.

If you are single, you must find someone—your parents, your best friend or a financial advisor with whom you can discuss your retirement plans. I know you can do it all on your own, but there are decisions you must make that will affect other people.

Throughout this book, I'll be talking mostly to married couples, but if you are single, just substitute the word "spouse" for "friend/ significant other/ parents" . . . whomever you choose to share your information and plans for retirement with. My reasoning is simple: I don't want to make reading this book cumbersome. I would certainly get tired of typing spouse/friend/significant other/parents/attorney/financial advisor" over and over. And I can only imagine your eyes rolling into the back of your head. So, simplicity. Enough said?

Why Should You Read This Book?

Am I trying to scare you? Maybe a little. Things usually don't turn out well for people who don't do ANY planning before making some sort of lifestyle change. Retirement planning is no different . . . and much more important. You must commit to planning prior to retiring.

Do you need this book? If you are a planner and feel you already have it all figured out, I encourage you to read through each chapter—at least skim through them. Perhaps you will find new sources of income you didn't originally take into account. At the very least, it won't hurt to validate your figures.

If you're NOT a planner but are expecting things to magically "work out", I REALLY encourage you to read this book. Here are some reasons you should pay close attention to this book:

1. There may be topics you've never considered that could mean new funds you can count on in retirement.

2. There will probably be some myths you have always believed that are completely false.

3. You may be basing your retirement on what someone has told you, not on your own research.

Planning for YOUR retirement is YOUR responsibility. Whether you do it yourself using this book and the worksheet or hire a financial advisor to do it for you, you still have to do the "up front" work—gathering information. The facts and figures the advisor needs are the same facts and figures I will be asking you to collect and use for your planning. Save yourself some money and at least go through this exercise once. Then, if you still need a financial advisor, he/she will be duly impressed that you have already done so much prep work.

What to Expect

In the following chapters, we are going to review the different types of retirement income and what may be available to you.

First up, we'll discuss Guaranteed Income: Social Security, pensions and annuities. This is income that is not dependent on your savings.

Then, we will discuss your Assets which include savings accounts, home equity, qualified and non-qualified retirement accounts.

After we've discussed Guaranteed Income and Assets, we'll cover how much you can safely withdraw from your accounts on an annual basis—without running out of money. Finally, we'll calculate an annual amount you can (reasonably) expect, and determine what your monthly income will be.

Before you get started, you should take a look at the workbook in the back of this book. You can also download it using the information in the Resources section of this book to get immediate access. By keeping a digital copy, you can revisit this book every year or so to make sure you're still on track . . . if you haven't retired yet.

Fill in amounts in the workbook section as you go. It will save you time later. Otherwise, you would have to go back through each chapter to figure out what goes in each section of the workbook. I highly recommend you use the workbook section, though. Seeing the bottom line after you do the work can be an eye-opener. Either you're on track to retire when you planned or you're not. In any case, by the time you finish this book, including the workbook, you'll have a pretty clear picture of what you need to do.

One more thing before you get started. You could sit down and read this book in one sitting, but it probably won't do you much good if you're not willing to take the time to think about each chapter and how it might impact your plan.

Will this be easy? Probably not. But if not now, then when?

Find a relaxing spot. Grab a pen and some paper and prepare to take a few notes.

Let's find out if you have planned for your best retirement.

Don't just retire . . .
Retire like you OWN it!!

Chapter 2 – Social Security

Social Security is a federal program (do you read "complicated" when you see the words "federal program"?) that provides income and health insurance to retired persons, the disabled, the poor, and other groups.

The program started in 1935 when the Social Security Act was signed. Because of the devastation of the Great Depression, the government was trying to provide a safety net for the millions of people who had suffered through it.

Today, most retirees are eligible for Social Security if they work long enough (the rules are outlined on the Social Security website). The subject of Social Security is so huge, it could fill volumes (and actually does).

The only part of Social Security we will address in this book pertains to retirees. We won't cover any of the other groups Social Security sometimes covers – disability, etc.

Social Security Tax

If you pay attention to your check stub each week/month, you probably already know that you pay Social Security taxes out of each paycheck. These taxes are assessed on all the wages you earn, up to a capped maximum. In 2018, the cap was $128,400. Employees are taxed at 6.2% of wages earned. If you earned the maximum taxable wages of $128,400, you would pay $7,960.80 in Social Security taxes over the course of the year. (If you earned more than $128,400 for 2018, your Social Security taxes would still be $7,960.80). Just so you know, the maximum taxable wages tend to go up each year (more taxes accumulated).

Your employer also pays Social Security taxes on your behalf—equal to the amount you pay. If you are self-employed, you must pay the full 12.4% of your salary for Social Security taxes.

This is the source of the Social Security you are able to withdraw when you reach retirement age.

Full-Benefit Retirement Age

Social Security's full-benefit retirement age is the earliest time when you can receive your full monthly benefit. Originally, the full benefit age was 65, but it has been increasing gradually be-cause of legislation passed by Congress in 1983. If you were born before 1955, your full-benefit re-tirement age is 66. Anyone born in 1955, will have to wait until 66 years and 2 months; in 1956, you must wait until age 66 and 4 months, etc. It is gradually rising to 67 for those born in 1960 or later.

Why do you think the government started pushing back the age to retire? My theory is someone woke up one day in the early 80's and said, "Hey, you know all those people who were born after World War II—the 'baby boomers'? They are going to start retiring in 2011 and there are millions of them". There was some panic, then some frantic calculations, and finally the realization that some-one had to do something. Fast. So, they came up with two ideas:

1. They would start raising the cap each year on how much of your earnings is subject to the Social Security tax.

2. They would start raising the full-benefit re-tirement age.

And that, my friends, is **my** version of your history lesson for today.

Early Retirement

Early retirement benefits are available at age 62. However, if you choose early retirement, there will be a permanent reduction of your benefit amount. If you wake up six months after beginning your early withdrawals and decide you want to wait un-til your full-benefit retirement age . . . too bad. Unless you are willing to pay back the six months of income you've already received, that just won't happen.

If you were born before 1955, your benefit will be 75% of your full benefit amount—for the rest of your life. As full benefit age continues to increase, your early benefits will also be impacted. When the full-benefit age reaches 67, benefits taken at age 62 will be reduced to 70 percent of the full benefit amount.

So, bottom line? Do your homework before you decide to start taking Social Security benefits.

Delayed Retirement

There is a financial bonus for delayed retirement. At the time this book was written, your full benefit amount continues to grow by 8% for each year you wait to retire (after your full benefit retirement age). This continues to accrue until the age of 70, after which there is no additional benefit of waiting to retire.

Marriage and Social Security

If you are married, you can collect retirement benefits based on your own earnings from work OR an amount equal to 50% of your spouse's retirement benefit (whichever is higher). Not both.

Example1: Mr. Smith receives a retirement benefit of $2000 a month. When his wife retires, her retirement, based on her work record, would be $800 per month. She could choose to receive the amount equal to 50% of her husband's benefit, which would be $1000 per month (larger than her work-related retirement amount.)

In this example, the couple would receive $3000 per month—Mr. Smith's $2000 and Mrs. Smith's $1000. This is more than the $2800 they would receive if Mrs. Smith had stuck with her $800 benefit.

If Mr. Smith dies first, Mrs. Smith will begin receiving **only** her husband's larger $2000 amount each month. If Mrs. Smith dies first, Mr. Smith would receive only his benefit of $2000 per month.

Example 2: If Mrs. Smith's work-related benefit was $1500, she would take her own benefit instead of the $1000 (50% of her husband's benefit). In that case, the couple would receive $3500 per month (Mr. Smith's $2000 + Mrs. Smith's $1500).

If Mr. Smith dies first, Mrs. Smith will begin receiving **only** her husband's larger $2000 amount each month. If Mrs. Smith dies first, Mr. Smith would receive only his benefit of $2000 per month.

Divorce and Social Security

How does divorce affect Social Security benefits? If you've been married for at least ten consecutive years and you're now single – you are in luck. You are eligible for the 50 percent spousal benefit even though you are now divorced. If your ex- dies, you can get the 100 percent survivor benefit if you're still single OR if you remarried after the age of 60.

Example 3: Mark and Sally Johnson were married fifteen years and are now divorced. Mark is drawing $2000 per month in Social Security benefits. Sally just retired. She is full-benefit retirement age, still single, and eligible for a benefit of 50% of Mark's monthly benefit - $1000 per month. When Mark dies, she can receive $2000 per month.

NOTE: If Sally was not yet full-benefit retirement age, she would receive less than 50% of Mark's benefit. Her amount would be decreased dependant on her age and she could not start receiving any benefit until she is at least 62.

Example 4: Sam and Sharon Smith were married twelve years, then divorced. Sam died last year after four years of retirement. His monthly Social Security benefit was $2000. Sharon remarried five years ago—when she was 61. Her new husband died this year after one year of retirement. She is now ready to retire and must make some decisions. Will she take her own benefit—$1500 per month, her second husband's death benefit—$1800, or Sam's death benefit ($2000)?

In this example, Sharon had to be married to her first husband at least 10 years, remarried after the age of 60, and is now full-benefit retirement age. Because she fulfilled all of the requirements, she is entitled to her own benefit or survivor benefits from either husband.

Complicated, right?

Your Own Social Security Account

Some of the rules are fairly complex, so you should check out your questions on the Social Security website (See Resources page). On this site you can find a LOT of information. It also provides a link where you can set up your own Social Security account. (Link is on the Resources page at the end of this book.) Once you set up your own account, you will be able to get personalized information about your retirement benefits—what you can expect to receive at different ages, beginning at age 62.

Your Social Security Work History

Once you set up your own account with Social Security, you can request reports containing your work history. I highly recommend you review this very carefully. If you find errors that could impact your benefits calculation, you should work to have them corrected before you retire. You owe it to yourself and your family to receive your maximum benefit amount after you retire.

NOTE: I also recommend you check out your local Social Security office. You can get the number online by searching for the office closest to your zip code. Often you will be able to get answers to your questions more quickly than calling the main SSA office. (This is definitely the route we take.)

You're welcome.

Chapter 3 – Pension Plans

Pensions are Defined Benefit plans (DBs). They guarantee a specific amount of monthly income in retirement.

Do you have a pension plan from where you work now or someplace you've worked in the past? If so, this can be a really sweet deal.

With a DB plan, your employer sets aside money into an investment pool and uses it to pay pension benefits to you once you retire. They use a formula which includes the number of years you have worked for the organization, your earnings and age. For example, your employer may promise you a pension benefit that's equal to one percent of your average salary over the last five years times your total years of employment with the company.

Example 1:

No. of Years at the company—25

Avg salary over past 5 years—$60,000

Calculation: 25*(60000 * .01) = $15,000/yr or $1250.00 per month.

With this type of plan, your employer is guaranteeing you'll receive a defined amount of money when you retire. The investment risk is on the plan provider (your organization), so regardless of how the investment pool performs, you should receive your pension each month.

Since the Enron financial crisis several years ago, there are many, many government regulations in place designed to protect employees with pensions.

In fact, unless your company goes entirely bankrupt, it's probably a pretty good bet that you're covered. Take your pension and be thankful.

Note: There aren't many pensions still offered by corporations. More often you will find them offered in the public sector – military, police, public education, city, county, state, etc.

About 37 percent of current retirees receive income from pensions.

Survivor Benefits

Be sure you understand how the funds will be paid out after you retire. You will usually have options which affect your monthly payment and your total benefit.

You and your spouse should discuss the options before you make a final decision. In many cases you will have these three choices:

1. You can take the whole amount in a lump sum. An amount will be calculated based on what you would have expected to receive over some period of time, for example, 5 years. You will be offered that amount which you can take and invest or do what you like. You will not receive any monthly payments during your lifetime. Nor will your spouse. You will owe taxes on the lump sum amount for the year in which you receive it.

   Using the example at the beginning of this chapter, you might receive $75,000 as one lump sum, but there will be no further payments – EVER.

2. You can choose to receive the full monthly amount calculated (based on your salary and number of years of service) each month until you die. When you die, the benefit ceases. Your surviving spouse will not receive any further benefits from your pension.

   For the example in this chapter, you will receive $1250 per month (pre-tax).

3. You can take a slightly decreased amount (than you would receive in #2 above) each month, but when you die, your surviving spouse will continue to receive the same pension amount each month until he/she

dies. Once both of you are gone, no payments will be made to any of your surviving
family.

Using this option, you might receive $1100
per month instead of $1250 for the rest of
your life. When you die, your surviving
spouse would continue to receive $1100 per
month until he/she dies.

All of these calculations will affect your "bottom
line" when doing your total retirement income calculations – which is one reason why I've included
this information. You must do the calculations
and determine if the additional cash flow will be
needed each month or if you can afford to take option 3 and guarantee an income for your spouse
after you are gone.

The choice is up to **you and your spouse**, even
though you will be the one signing the papers. It's
one of those "communication" topics that is criti-
cal to a happy life together. Trust me on this. Talk
it out—together!

So . . . if you are eligible for a pension, is it enough
to finance your retirement? Perhaps when you add
in Social Security, it will be enough for you to "retire", but you probably won't be doing any of those
extra things on your list. In other words, it won't
be the retirement of your dreams.

Don't stop here—let's keep going to see if there are
other sources of income you can expect when you
retire.

Chapter 4 – Annuities

An annuity is an insurance product that pays out income. It can be one part of your retirement strategy.

You invest in an annuity, either one lump payment or a series of payments, then it makes payments to you at a future date. You can elect to take out a lump sum payment or a series of payments over time (monthly, quarterly or annually). Usually you must wait 5–7 years after funding the annuity before starting withdrawals. Ideally, you should plan ahead and purchase the annuity long before you plan to retire or need the money.

The size of your payments is determined by a variety of factors, including the length of your payout period.

You can choose to receive payments for the rest of your life, or for a set number of years. How much you receive depends on several factors:

1. How long you wish to receive payments

2. Whether you've chosen a guaranteed payout (fixed annuity) or a payment determined by the performance of your annuity's underlying investments (variable annuity).

Annuities allow you to defer paying taxes on the amount you paid into the annuity. However, if you take an early withdrawal, you will pay surrender charges - maybe 7% of your investment or more. Annuities often charge higher fees overall:

1. an upfront commission (as much as 10% of your investment)

2. ongoing investment management fees and other fees

The fees alone can amount to as much as 2 - 3% of your investment per year.

If you are considering an annuity, make sure that you ask a LOT of questions and carefully review the fine print first.

Survivor Benefits

The person who purchases the annuity is the annuitant. Anyone can be assigned as the beneficiary of the annuity when the annuitant dies. Usually it is a parent or spouse of the deceased. Beneficiaries typically have three main options to receive annuity payments after the owner's death:

1. Lump Sum Distribution: the beneficiary will receive the designated funds as a lump sum amount.

2. Non-Qualified Stretch: the beneficiary will receive minimum payments stretched over their life expectancy.

3. Five-Year Rule: the beneficiary can withdraw amounts during a five-year period or withdraw the entire sum in the fifth year.

Communication

You and your spouse (or designated beneficiary) should discuss payout options with the insurance company before purchasing the annuity.

Not only does it get you both on the same page financially, it is a great gift to people you love to help them understand the overall financial picture of your family. Whatever you do, make sure that when you die, your loved ones are NOT left clueless about what to do and what the financial future looks like for them.

Okay, enough said.

Chapter 5 – Misc Sources

Bank Accounts & CDs

If you have large bank accounts or certificates of deposit (CDs), consider these as part of your retirement income. They can certainly be used to hold some of your "liquid assets". Some investment specialists suggest retirees keep a substantial amount of their living expenses—as much as two to four years of income—outside the stock market . . . in a bank account or CD.

Of course, not all of us (actually not many of us) have two to four years of income sitting anywhere, and especially not in a savings account that pays less than 1% interest (at the time of writing this book). But usually you can earn more interest with CD's than with bank accounts.

Be aware of all your bank accounts and their balances. You can determine if they will/should play a role in your retirement planning.

If Your Home is Paid Off

If your home is paid off but you fear not having enough income in your retirement, there are options available to you.

1. Home Equity Loan
2. Reverse Mortgage
3. Rental Income

Home Equity

Even though you have equity in your home, lenders seem to make it difficult for retirees to qualify for a home equity loan. Many lenders use W2's from your tax returns to validate your income. Once you retire most of your income will generate 1099's. Lenders don't seem to have made that leap in thinking, yet. From personal experience, I suggest if you plan to apply for one, do so while you are **both still** working.

If you do qualify for one, you can use the cash from the home equity loan to help out during an emergency situation. It would also be beneficial if the stock market is in crisis and you don't want to pull money out of your investments until the market improves. You may find it beneficial to have this money put aside.

In any case, you will probably have to make payments on the loan, but the money put aside can still be a lifesaver if you need quick cash and you happen to have it stashed in your checking account.

This might also allow you to stay in your home longer, if this is something you really want to ensure.

Reverse Mortgage

If you have your home completely paid off or nearly so, and want to stay in your home but are short on cash each month, you might consider a reverse mortgage. This is a loan against your home with no payments due until you die, sell your home, or leave it permanently (i.e. go into a nursing home).

A reverse mortgage is a loan available to homeowners who are 62 years or older. It allows them to convert part of the equity in their homes to cash. It was designed to allow retirees to continue to live in their existing home after retirement, using the accumulated wealth in their homes to cover basic monthly living expenses and pay for health care. But you can use the proceeds of the loan any way you choose.

Instead of making monthly payments to a lender, the lender makes payments to the borrower (retired couple).

As long as the borrower lives in the home, he/she is not required to pay back the loan until the home is sold. The borrower must remain current on property taxes, homeowner's insurance and homeowner's association dues (if applicable).

The final debt is usually settled from the proceeds of the sale of your home. The costs are high, though, with fees usually higher than with a traditional mortgage.

There are cons to reverse mortgages, though.

1. The loan balance increases over time as interest on the loan and fees accumulate.

2. As your home equity is used, there are fewer assets to leave to your heirs. You can still leave the home to them, but they will have to repay the loan balance. Usually the loan balance is paid off by selling the home.

3. Your eligibility for Medicaid or Supplemental Security Income (SSI) may be affected. You should consult a benefits specialist if you are considering this option.

You will see a lot of celebrities endorse reverse mortgages. Please see a financial advisor before taking this step. They may be able to suggest a different (better) option than a reverse mortgage.

Rental Income

If you need additional income and are determined not to leave or sell your home, you might consider taking in a renter. This would provide some companionship if you are alone. In any case, the income might be welcome.

If you don't mind leaving your home because you are downsizing or moving to another area, you might consider renting your home. There are younger families who need the space you no longer need. If you have paid it off and own free and clear, the rent would help fund your retirement. In most cases, you can rent it for more than you would spend for rent in an apartment or the payment for another (smaller) home—if you decided to downsize.

What if Your home is not paid off?

If your home is not paid off when you retire, which will probably be the case for many retirees, there are options.

1. Stay where you are and do nothing

2. Refinance your home for a lower monthly payment

3. Rent your home to someone else and downsize to an apartment

4. Sell your home

You can . . . Stay where you are and do nothing

There isn't much to say here. If you can afford your monthly house payment and upkeep, you change nothing.

Or . . . Refinance and stay where you are

If your monthly payment is too high for comfort, you might consider refinancing your home for a lower payment. There are a lot of "ifs" to consider, though. **If** the new interest rate you can get is lower than the one you have now; **if** you have enough equity in your house; **if** you are still employed or **if** the mortgage company will even discuss refinancing after you are retired; and **if** the monthly payment will actually be lower than what you now pay, considering the closing costs they tack on to your "new" loan.

In the previous section, I explained under Home Equity that many lenders have a problem giving credit to retirees because they don't have any W2's. At tax time, you will find only 1099's in your mail box for all the funds you received during the year (if you were not an employee of a company). Apparently, lenders are having a hard time understanding that people do get paid by 1099's. My advice is to plan early and apply for refinancing before you retire.

Or . . . Rent your home out and downsize

If you want to hold on to your home but find it too large for you now, consider renting it to a younger family. They will appreciate the additional space for their growing kids and you will appreciate not having to clean the larger home.

If you are holding onto the larger home as an inheritance for your children and have the funds, you can purchase a smaller home.

If the rent you are receiving offsets the mortgage payments and you don't want to purchase another home, you could rent an apartment or a smaller home.

Or . . . Sell your home

If you decide to sell your home and downsize, you have many options. You could stay in the same area and rent or purchase another home. You could move to another city, state or country.

Make sure you do a lot of research before you decide to move away from family and friends, though. It's much more expensive to correct your mistake if you move 2000 miles away and decide after six months you don't like your new location or feel you need to be with family again.

Chapter 6 – Qualified Plans

A **qualified plan** is simply one that is described in Section 401(a) of the Tax Code. You and/or your company contributes to your plan. Usually, your contributions are not taxed until you withdraw money from the plan.

Qualified plans are also known as **Defined Contribution** (DC) retirement plans. They provide a way for you to save a certain percentage of each paycheck towards retirement. Your contributions are usually taken out before tax which reduces your taxable amount (therefore lowering the tax percentage you pay at end of year). There are several types of retirement plans, depending on the type of organization for which you work(ed).

I've listed some of the more common types of plans in this chapter.

401(k)

A 401(k) is probably the most common DC plan. It is usually offered by for-profit organizations, such as corporations. These plans are popular with **employers** because they are less expensive than other types of retirement plans. Contributions are one of the largest expenses for an employer. But in the case of a 401(k) plan, most of the contributions are made by the employee.

An employee makes regular contributions from their paycheck (each payday) and defers the income. This simply means they will wait until retirement to withdraw those funds from their 401(k) account.

There are many rules associated with DC plans, but there are also many benefits. These plans are popular with **employees** because the plan allows them to save for retirement while also reducing their current income tax bill. They aren't taxed on the funds in the retirement plan until retirement or some type of withdrawal is made. Employers usually allow employees to change the amount of salary deferred into the plan as the employees' circumstances change. Also, employees are frequently given access to their retirement funds through loans or hardship withdrawals.

Where does the money go?

The money you contribute goes into your 401(k) account which is held by your company until you leave the company. Sometimes organizations will contract with a third-party holding company to hold, invest and report the funds you contribute to your 401(k).

Choosing how to invest the funds in your 401(k) account is generally your responsibility. Your company will generally offer you a mixture of mutual funds and bond funds from which to choose. Your decisions should be based on research of each of the funds in the list you've been provided. There are many websites that will provide in-depth information about each fund—how it has performed over a period of time, which stocks or bonds make up the fund, its risk, and many other characteristics you should consider.

Depending on your age and your risk aversion, you must decide whether to put your money in bond funds (very conservative), mutual funds (a little riskier since they are tied to the stock market), a combination of the two, or any variety of other types of funds. You may have answered some questions about how you handle risk when you signed up for your 401(k). If not, you can check online for risk calculators. Both you and your spouse should take that test to determine the level of risk with which you are comfortable. It's very possible that you have two different attitudes about risk. Communication is key here.

Company Match

When your company chooses to contribute to your plan, you benefit from "free money." Many companies **match** a percentage of the total amount you contribute each year. It is a great incentive to help people contribute to their own retirement plan. This has, in most cases replaced the DB (Pension Plan) option.

How Company Match Works

When the company decides to implement a match program, it will define how much it will contribute. This percentage amount usually remains constant each year. As an example, a company may decide to **match** up to 3% of each employee's salary as a contribution to their plan.

If you, as an employee, contribute at least 3% each year to your retirement plan, the company will match your contribution – up to 3%. If you contribute 5%, the company will still contribute 3%. **But if you contribute nothing, neither will they**.

There should be no question in your mind whether you should contribute to your retirement plan. The only question is how much. If possible, try to contribute the maximum allowed by law each year. You are allowed to contribute up to $19,000 per year (as of 2019 tax rules) to your retirement plan. Employer contributions do not count toward the annual limit.

Note: If you are over age 50 you can make $6000 additional catch-up contributions to your retirement plan each year. That makes a total of $25,000 you can contribute. Yea!

If things are really tight in your budget, make a commitment to contribute a portion of your next raise to your retirement plan. For example, if you receive a 2% raise, start contributing 1% of your salary to the plan. The company will match that 1% and you end up with 2% in your retirement plan at the end of the first year. Keep this up and you will begin to see huge changes in your plan's balance year after year.

Here are some examples to help explain employer match:

Example 1: ABC Company announced a match program for employees contributing to their 401(k) plan. They will match the first 5% any employee contributes at a 100% rate.

Sue Smith works for ABC Company and contributes 10% of the gross amount of her paycheck each month. ABC Company will deposit an amount to match 5% of Sue's gross amount each month. Her 10% plus the company's 5% means an amount equal to 15% of Sue's gross paycheck amount is deposited in her 401(k) each month. Huge win since she is only contributing 10% of that total amount. Free money! Who doesn't like that?

Example 2: Harry Johnson also works for ABC Company. Harry contributes only 3% of his paycheck's gross amount each month. ABC Company will match the 3% that Harry is contributing, making a total of 6% being deposited in Harry's 401(k) each month.

   Example 3: Sue Smith turned 50 last year and wants to contribute extra to her 401(k) now. She will contribute an extra $500 per month in addition to the 10% she already contributes (see example 1). She must reach the maximun amount allowable for the contribution year ($19,000 in 2019) before her extra $500 per month counts as a catch-up contribution.

   Example 4: Sam Johnson works for ABC Company, but he does not contribute to a 401(k). ABC Company will **not** contribute to Sam's 401(k).

Vesting

Based on how long you have been with the company, you may be able to take all or only a percentage of the company's match funds deposited in your 401(k) account. Vesting schedules usually apply to any money the company contributes. You must contact your current company to get details about the vesting schedule they use. Bottom line—know what your company's vesting schedule is and make sure you stay until you're fully vested if you want to receive 100% of the company profit-sharing in your account.

Profit Sharing

Profit sharing is a contribution to employees that the company decides to make, usually after the end of the tax year. The contributions are tax deductible for employers.

Employers assess their finances at the end of the year before deciding whether they want to make a one-time contribution to each employee. As an employee, you receive bonus compensation, tax-deferred, and your employer has the flexibility to choose how big of a contribution they want to make (if they want to make one at all).

The calculation usually goes something like this: The company decides to give each employee 3% of their annual salary as profit sharing. If you make $50,000 annually, the company would deposit $1500.00 in your profit-sharing account. There is some controversy over how companies calculate and distribute profit sharing. Each company has its own method, but bottom-line? You get more "free money"!

This is a huge win for you! But here's the thing: just like with company matching, vesting schedules apply. As with company match, make sure you know what your company's vesting schedule is and plan to stay until you're fully vested if you want to receive 100% of the company profit-sharing in your account.

What Happens When You Retire?

When you are ready to retire, you must then decide what to do with your 401(k) account. In most cases, the company from which you retired will not be the one making payments to you from your account after retirement. Your most likely path will be to do a rollover into an IRA.

You can **roll over** the entire 401(k) account to a 3rd party company like Fidelity, Voya, or a hundred other companies that would love to have the opportunity to manage your 401(k) account. Once you roll over your 401(k) or any qualified plan to a third-party company, your money will be in an IRA account. This is simply an account which holds pre-tax money until you decide to take withdrawals. These companies will invest your money in the way you designate (see the previous section, Where Does Your Money Go) and keep you informed of the balance of your account monthy and/or quarterly. You will have access online to track your account and make investment changes when you like.

You can also go the "personal" route and choose a financial advisor to control your investments and keep you advised on the health and status of your account. A financial advisor will have fiduciary responsibility to you. This means the advisor will act entirely on your behalf and best interest. There is a legal responsibility there. That said, it's still best if you interview several financial advisors before putting your life savings in someone's hands. Ask questions about what type of investments they handle—do they invest only in funds where they have a vested interest? If so, run away as fast as you can. In any case, you must be able to trust anyone who is handling your life savings. Talk to friends. Get suggestions. Set up interviews. Remember . . . we are talking about YOUR LIFE savings.

What you need to know about Rollovers

Before we go on, humor me just a moment. Permit me to remind you of a very word I used a couple of paragraphs back—**ROLLOVER/Roll Over**. This is an important word to remember any time you are discussing moving your account from one company to another. You must ROLL OVER your funds. **Do not MOVE them**. This is relevant after you retire and choose another company to handle your account. It is also important if you decide to move from one company to another after you have an IRA set up.

Why is this important? As long as you are rolling over funds, you do not have to pay taxes. If you take any of your retirement funds out of your account, you WILL pay taxes. If you **MOVE** the funds from one company to another, you will receive a check in the mail with the amount you are moving minus 10% tax the company takes out. It will be up to you to send the $90,000 to the new company plus the 10% ($10,000) that went to pay taxes if you don't want to pay taxes on a $100,000 distribution. (The IRS sees the MOVE as a distribution, not a rollover).

Here is an example of how it SHOULD go:

Example 5: Frank retired from ABC Company. He had $100,000 in his 401(k). He chose LMN Company to hold his money in an IRA. He set up the IRA account and told LMN he wanted to ROLL OVER his funds from ABC. LMN handled the transaction and the funds were sent to LMN. When Frank was notified the transaction was complete, he saw $100,000 in his IRA account at LMN. He never touched the money. It was all handled by LMN and ABC. He paid NO taxes on the rollover.

You do not want to go down the road with the MOVE scenario. Let's just say, it will be a big, hot mess and you will never forget that lesson.

Still confused? Just ask questions when you are ready to transfer funds from one place to another and DO NOT forget the word "ROLLOVER". It will save you a lot of heartache in the long run.

RMDs

One of the things people don't talk about a lot is how much money you can / should / must take out of your account each year after you retire.

Until you reach the age of 70 ½, you can take out any amount you like. Once you hit that magical age of 70 ½, though, the government defines the minimum you can take out of your account each year until you die. This is called the Required Minimum Distribution (RMD).

According to the government, you must deplete your retirement funds by the time you are 115. Because of that, there is a very specific calculation for each year after you turn 70 1/2. We found there are some things that are unclear about calculating RMD.

1. You must do the calculation at the **beginning** of each year to determine what your RMD amount will be for that year. (At the beginning of 2019, you are doing the calculations for 2019).

2. You must use the ending balance or your retirement account (probably an IRA at this point) at the end of the prior year (end of 2018 if doing the calculation for 2019).

3. Use your age at the end of the current year (2019 if calculating for 2019).

Example 6: Sally Sandstone will be 71 at the end of this year, 2019. On January 4, 2019, she received her IRA year-end statement dated 12/31/2018. Using her balance at the end of 2018 and her age at the end of 2019, she calculated the total amount of her RMD. She divided that amount by 12, to know how much she needed to take out of her account each month.

You can find RMD charts everywhere online which you can use to ensure you are taking out the correct amount. You can also find that information on the Social Security website.

NOTE 1: If you have more than one retirement account, you must add the total value of each of them at the end of the previous year to divide by the RMD percentage from the rate chart. (This amount should not include your Guaranteed Income). IRS does not care which of your accounts you take the money from to satisfy the RMD for that year. They just care that you take the right amount.

NOTE 2: You do NOT want to forget about RMD and take out too little one year. The tax penanties are extremely high – like 50% and IRS will never forget your name. I don't know about you, but I don't want to ever be on their "BAD" list.

Survivor's Benefits

You are required to designate a beneficiary for your 401(k) when you set it up. Don't forget who you named as beneficiary. Your new spouse will not be enthused to find out your ex- is still listed as the beneficiary on your 401(k).

Your beneficiary will take ownership of your account when you die. It is transferred to their name and they will be responsible for making any further decisions about investments—working with the institution where the funds are currently invested, of course. It is also the beneficiary's option to transfer those funds or do whatever they want with the money in the account. The government (IRS) will have rules and the institution will make sure those are followed.

Solo 401(k)

The Solo 401(k) plan is an IRS approved qualified 401(k) plan (DC) designed for a self- employed individual or the sole owner-employee of a corporation and their spouse. The rules of a Solo 401(k) are basically the same as those for a regular 401(k), except the funds you contribute are not taken out of your paycheck each month.

The business owner wears two hats in a 401(k) plan: employee and employer. Contributions can be made to the plan in both capacities.

403(b)

A 403(b) plan, is a DC retirement plan for specific employees of public schools, tax-exempt organizations and certain ministers. These plans can invest in either annuities or mutual funds. A 403(b)plan is another name for a tax-sheltered annuity (TSA) plan.

Individual accounts in a 403(b) plan can be any of the following types:

1. An annuity contract, which is a contract provided through an insurance company.

2. A custodial account, which is an account invested in mutual funds.

3. A retirement income account set up for church employees. Generally, retirement income accounts can invest in either annuities or mutual funds.

The benefits for contributing to a 403(b) are similar to those for contributing to a 401(k):

1. The first benefit is that you don't pay income tax on allowable contributions until you begin making withdrawals from the plan, usually after you retire. Allowable contributions to a 403(b) plan are either excluded or deducted from your income.

2. The second benefit is that earnings and gains on amounts in your 403(b) account aren't taxed until you withdraw them.

Note. Generally, employees must pay social security and Medicare tax on their contributions to a 403(b) plan, including those made under a salary reduction agreement.

The same contribution limit that applies for 401(k) ($19,000 per year in 2019) applies for 403(b) also.

457

The 457 plan is a type of non-qualified, tax-advantaged DC retirement plan that is available for some state and local governments as well as certain non-governmental employers in the United States. The employer provides the plan and the employee defers compensation into it on a pre-tax or after-tax (Roth) basis.

The same contribution limit that applies for 401(k) and 403(b) ($19,000 per year in 2019) applies for 457 also.

Please Note: For 403(b) and 457 plans, much of the information provided for the 401(k) also applies. Choosing the funds into which you will invest your retirement funds, Vesting, RMD, Rollovers, and Survivor Benefits are all basically the same.

What if you've worked multiple places?

If you have worked for multiple companies and had multiple retirement plans to which you contributed, your juggling days are over. You can handle the funds from the previous organization(s) by rolling them into your plan at the company where you now work. No more setting up spreadsheets with all your retirement plans listed and trying to keep track of everything.

Another option is to open an IRA with an investment firm (like Fidelity, etc.) and roll everything from the old companies into one account. This generally gives you many more investing options than your employer offers for your retirement plan. You can make your own investment decisions or even have a representative adviser assigned to you if your account is large enough. The investing / adviser rules differ from firm to firm.

Just so we're clear, you can't move your funds from your current employer to a third-party investment firm. Do your research to see which would be more beneficial: rolling your older plans into your current plan, or rolling them into an IRA.

You may find that your current plan is superior to any of the older plans. For example, my husband's 457 plan offered a guaranteed 4% return for his retirement funds. He rolled a couple of previous plans into that one and now we have a guaranteed rate for everything in that account. WIN!!

One thing you **must** remember – there is no co-mingling of funds. Ever. That means if you have a 401(k), a 457 and a 403(b), the funds will always be kept separate. When you retire, you can roll over all three into one IRA, but the funds will be kept separate within the IRA. When you start to take distributions after you retire, you can elect to take funds from your IRA. You can specify which of your accounts / funds the distributions should come from.

What if you're married?

Contributing to your retirement plan(s) has no bearing on your spouse's plan(s). Remember the "no comingling" rule I mentioned previously? That goes doubly for you and your spouse. Your funds will be in one IRA under your name and your spouse's will be in a different IRA account. Any distributions from accounts the two of you have—IRA, pension, etc. will be deposited separately into your checking or savings account each month. The only time your funds will be in the same account is when one of you dies. Then the other person will receive the proceeds from the deceased's account (hopefully as a rollover or whatever terminology the government uses at that time), and the amount of distributions that must be taken will be recalculated.

Chapter 7 – Non-Qualified and Misc Plans

Non-Qualified Plans

A **non-qualified plan** is a type of tax-deferred, employer-sponsored retirement plan that is not under the employee retirement income security act guidelinesn (401(k), 457, etc.). Non-qualified plans are typically designed for key executives and other select employees.

There are four major types of non-qualified plans:

1. deferred-compensation plans

2. executive bonus plans

3. group carve-out plans

4. split-dollar life insurance plans

The contributions made to these plans are usually nondeductible to the employer and taxable to the employee, which doesn't exactly sound like a win-win. However, they allow employees to defer taxes until retirement—when they are presumably in a lower tax bracket. Non-qualified plans are often used to provide specialized forms of compensation to key executives or employees in place of making them partners or part owners in the company or corporation.

They are often used by employers as an attraction and retention vehicle—an NQDC plan is more like an agreement between you and your employer to defer a portion of your annual income until a specific date in the future. Depending on the plan, that date could be in 5 years, 10 years, or in retirement. For example, you could defer compensation to cover shorter-term goals like paying a child's college tuition.

NQDC plans allow executives to defer a much larger portion of their compensation, and to defer taxes on the money until the deferral is paid. You should consider contributing to a NQDC plan only if you are maxing out your qualified plan options, such as a 401(k).

Misc Plans

Misc Plans don't fall under Qualified or Non-Qualified plans, but they are still considered Retirement plans.

IRA

An individual retirement account (IRA) is an investing tool used by individuals to earn and earmark funds for retirement savings.

It is an account set up at a financial institution that allows you to save for retirement with tax-free growth or on a tax-deferred basis.

Except for rollovers from an existing retirement plan, any funds you contribute to an IRA are after-tax and will be kept separate from any pre-tax money in the IRA. You can generally deduct a certain portion of the amount you contribute to your IRA each year when calculating federal taxes. For 2019, the limit is $6000.00 ($7,000.00 if you are 50 or older).

Because of tax implications when you begin to take money out of the IRA, all funds must be tracked separately. For example, since your retirement funds, like a 401(k), are pre-tax, you haven't paid tax on those funds – but you will when you withdraw them during retirement.

In all cases, you'll pay tax on the dividends earned on the amount you contributed – for your qualified, non-qualified and miscellaneous plans.

SEP IRA

A Simplified Employee Pension Individual Retirement Arrangement (SEP IRA) is a variation of the

IRA used in the United States. Business owners adopt these plans to provide retirement benefits for themselves and their employees. It is a simple, tax-deferred retirement plan for anyone who is self-employed, owns a business, employs others, or earns freelance income.

It is a traditional IRA and follows the same investment, distribution, and rollover rules as traditional IRA.

Simple IRA

A Savings Incentive Match Plan for Employees Individual Retirement Account ("SIMPLE IRA"), is a type of tax-deferred DC employer-provided retirement plan in the United States. It is usually offered within small businesses that have 100 or fewer employees.

It allows employees and employers to contribute to traditional IRAs set up for employees. It is ideally suited as a start-up retirement savings plan for small employers not currently sponsoring a retirement plan.

Roth IRA

A Roth IRA is a DC retirement plan under US law. It bears many similarities to the traditional IRA. The biggest distinction between the two is how they're taxed.

Traditional IRA contributions are generally made with pretax dollars; you usually get a tax deduction on your contribution and pay income tax when you withdraw the money from the account during retirement. Conversely, Roth IRAs are funded with after-tax dollars; the contributions are not tax deductible – although you may be able to take a tax credit of 10 to 50% of the contribution, depending on your income and life situation. But when you start withdrawing funds, qualified distributions are tax free.

If you have questions about any of the Misc Retirement Plans discussed so far in this section, please contact a tax attorney or a CPA or someone who can help you discern which, if any of these plans might work for you and/or your employees.

Whole Life with Cash Value

Cash-value life insurance is being included in the Miscellaneous section. This type of life insurance includes a death benefit and cash value accumulation. It differs from term life in that term life does not have any cash value.

Once you have accumulated a sizeable cash value, you can use these funds to:

- Pay your policy premium
- Take out a loan, sometimes at a lower rate than banks offer

- Create an investment portfolio that maintains and accumulates wealth

- Supplement retirement income *

This should not be considered a stream of income when you retire, but might get you over a rough bump if needed.

Note: Any withdrawal over the policy basis is taxable income during the year it is withdrawn.

* You should also know that if you take a withdrawal and not a loan, the company will close out your policy and it will be considered a distribution. So, make sure that is what you want to do. FYI, you will receive the cash value amount, but will forfeit the death benefit of the policy (the term portion). If that is not your goal, a loan might be the better option.

Chapter 8 – Withdrawals

How much can you withdraw when you retire?

In most cases, your guaranteed income alone will not be enough for you to live comfortably in retirement. If you want to be able to do any of the things you dreamed of doing, you will need some supplemental income. That's where your retirement savings can come into play.

Until you reach the age of 70 ½, **you** determine how much you are comfortable taking as a distribution each year from your investments to supplement your income. (See the RMD section under 401(k) in chapter 6.

But, the big question is how much can you **reasonably** expect to withdraw from your retirement plan each year without running out of money before you die?

The general rule of thumb has always been 4%. But honestly, the answer is: "it depends".

Yeah, not exactly what you wanted to hear. It would be so much simpler if we just had the "EASY" button. What "they" never tell you is it's NOT easy. You need to take several things into account before you come up with that magical amount. And, just so we're clear here, whatever percentage we use this year may change next year, the year after, and even the year after that.

Again . . . not what you want to hear.

But I want to make sure you have the information you need to live your retirement your way, not based on someone else's idea of what it should be like.

So, here goes.

Traditionally, "they" have always said that you can withdraw 4% per year from your retirement funds and not run out of money before you die.

But that's not necessarily true. Several factors come into play, like the stock market health, your age and RMD. In a perfect world, the stock market would always make money for you and the government wouldn't want you to run out of money by the time you're 115 years old.

In a perfect world, you could take out as much as you want every year. But . . . since we live in the real world, the percentage of your retirement funds you withdraw each year in retirement depends on these factors:

1. Your age. If you are at least 70 ½, the government determines the percentage you will withdraw each year based on your RMD calculation. (You have no control over this if you want to stay on the right side of the IRS).

2. How the market is doing. If the market is doing well, you may feel comfortable withdrawing more, knowing that your account is also doing well. If the market is doing poorly, well . . .

3. Your risk strategy / tolerance

Stock Market Risk

All investments involve some degree of risk. Don't let anyone tell you anything different. But with risk, there is usually some form of reward.

When it comes to investing, risk and reward go hand in hand. "No pain, no gain" fairly describes the relationship between risk and reward. If you plan to buy securities – such as stocks, bonds, mutual funds, or Exchange-Traded Funds (ETFs)—it is important that you understand you could lose some or all of the money you invest.

The reward for taking on risk is the potential for a greater investment return. An "aggressive" investor is willing to risk losing money to get potentially better results.

An "average" investor would include a large percentage of Americans who are investing in the stock market. Average investors see the wisdom of being in the market because of the potential for gains, but also has a healthy aversion for risk, so is not very keen on risky investing.

A "conservative" investor, or one with a low risk tolerance, favors investments that maintain his or her original investment. The aversion for risk is so high, the very thought of being in the stock market is unnerving. The conservative or risk averse investor loses a lot of sleep over what the market is doing.

Your Risk Tolerance

When you signed up for your 401(k), you might have been asked to answer questions which helped determine your risk tolerance. If you've never figured out your comfort level with investing, many investment websites offer free online questionnaires to help you assess your risk tolerance. Some of the websites will even estimate asset allocations based on responses to the questionnaires.

Bottom line . . . do you identify with one of the three categories? Do you feel you are an aggressive, average or conservative investor? Why is that important? How you have felt about the stock market and how comfortable you are investing will have a great deal to do with how you will choose to take distributions from your retirement funds.

For example, if you are more aggressive in the stock market and feel that overall your investments are doing very well, you could take out 5% per year. Being the savy investor you are, you realize you will need to cut back on your percentage in the years the market is not doing as well, but you are comfortable with that.

If you still have 10-20 years before you retire, you might consider yourself an aggressive investor. You anticipate making even more money by carefully investing in higher risk assets, such as stocks.

If you are traditional or an average investor, you understand the risks of the stock market and are fairly comfortable having your assets invested there. Depending on how close to retirement you are (within 2 – 5 years), you have probably adjusted your investments so they are more closely balanced, close to 50% in stocks and 50% in bonds. If the market is doing well, you will feel comfortable calculating your withdrawals at a 4% rate. You know there may be ups and downs in the market and are prepared to make a few adjustments if necessary.

If you are a conservative investor or are worried about investing in the stock market at all, you will have some decisions to make. You might still leave your investments in the stock market, but should probably calculate your withdrawals as low as 3%. You may even decide to move more funds to cash investments and/or low-risk mutual funds like money-market accounts.

Things Change

Just remember . . . your risk tolerance should (and probably will) change over the years—especially as you get closer to retirement age. In addition, your risk tolerance and that of your spouse may be completely different. You must decide how to compromise so you are both comfortable with your investing philosophy and risk tolerance.

Once you retire, you MUST pay attention to the market. That doesn't mean that you have to spend every minute worrying, but it does mean that you should be aware of market trends. If the stock market appears to be heading into a "bear" market (stock prices are down and your accounts seem to be losing money), you should consider cutting back on the percentage you are taking out each month.

If, on the other hand, the market is doing GREAT (bull market), you might consider taking out a bit more. Maybe you can finally take that cruise you've always wanted to take. That is entirely up to you and your financial advisor.

Keep your risk percentage in mind. You will need it when you do your final calculations in the next chapter.

Seek help if you need it

As in previous chapters, I suggest you seek out investment advice from a professional if you do not want to take on the responsibility of watching out for your investments. In addition, if you feel you don't understand the stock market at all and just don't feel comfortable being in it, a financial advisor or investment professional can suggest other ways to keep your money safe and take the worry off your shoulders. There is no shame in saying, "I don't understand."

Be very careful in choosing that professional, though. Uncle Bob or your neighbor's niece's husband may sound like the perfect person for the job, but please be careful. Some financial advisors have a vested interest in specific stocks/funds because they receive higher commissions or bonuses. Tread carefully, my friend. Ask questions. Listen for your "spidey" sense or B.S. detector—whatever you call it.

Can you smell a fraud? If so, run away. Run away faster.

Chapter 9 - Calculations

Ready to do "the work"?

If you have scanned this book without thinking through each of the chapters, now is the time to go back and do the work.

There is a link in the Resources section of this book for a <u>worksheet</u> you can use for your calculations. Download and print the worksheet, or if you don't have access to a printer you can use a sheet of paper to write out all the items that pertain to your retirement income. Group them together according to the information in each chapter of this book.

Step 1 - Guaranteed Income

Make a list of each of the sources of guaranteed income – Social Security, Pensions and annuities and any net rental income – from chapters 2-5. Next to each source, write down the annual amount you expect from each one. Total your guaranteed income to get **Annual Guaranteed Income**.

Step 2 – Assets

A. List your savings and investments (see chapters 6, 7). Next to each source, write down the total amount in each account.

   NOTE: You can write down the current value in your retirement account or you can estimate what the value would be at retirement based on the percentage of your income you are currently contributing.

B. Subtotal your assets from savings, 401(k), etc. This is your **Spendable Assets** total.

C. Calculate your cash cushion. We all need a cushion – the kind that protects you in emergency situations. Some experts suggest one- or two- years' worth of expenses that wouldn't be covered by your guaranteed income. If you know what your current annual budget is or what you anticipate it to be when you retire, then you know if your guaranteed income is going to meet your budget needs. If some of your expenses are not met by guaranteed income, you need to take that amount and multiply by 2 to get the two years of cash cushion you need.

D. Subtract the cash cushion you calculated in (C) from your Spendable Assets (B) to get your **Net Spendable Assets**.

E. Remember that percentage you were supposed to write down in chapter 8? Either 0.03, 0.04 or 0.05, depending on how much risk you are willing to take in the stock market with your retirement accounts. Now you will multiple your **Net Spendable Assets** (from D) by that percentage amount. This gives you the **Annual Income from Assets**.

Step 3 – Annual Income Calculation

Add **Annual Guaranteed Income** (Step 1) to **Annual Income from Assets (E)** for **Total Annual Income**.

Step 4 – Monthly Income

Divide the **Total Annual Income (See 3 above)** by 12 for the **Total Monthly Income**. This is the monthly income you can use for your budget calculations.

And you're done!

With the calculations, anyway. It wasn't too difficult, was it? It does require gathering a lot of paperwork and making sure you haven't forgotten anything. Start thinking about all the companies you or your spouse have worked for. Make sure you didn't leave funds someplace when you left. Don't forget Matching and Company Profit Sharing.

If you are still several years from retirement, keep a copy of the worksheet you just finished and plan to revisit the numbers annually to make sure you are on track for retirement.

If you are very close to retirement, you can use these calculations to compare to your budget. Do the figures work? What needs to change if they don't?

It's up to you, now. Start dreaming about your perfect retirement.

Resource Guide

1. Social Security website: https://www.ssa.gov/

2. Set up your own Social Security account:
 https://www.ssa.gov/myaccount/

3. Worksheet for Calculations
 https://pages.convertkit.com/2d787b166d/54a6abda4e

4. Retired Living Today website
 https://retiredlivingtoday.com

Thank You!

You made it to the end . . . YAY! I want to personally thank you for purchasing this book and reading it.

I hope you've gained some insight into planning for retirement. It isn't rocket science, but sometimes it can feel like it before you get started – it's a complicated subject. This book was designed to give you some basic information and help you understand different sources of income you might have in retirement.

I know all your questions haven't been answered, but this was a starting point. You will still have some investigation to do on your own. Contact your current and past employers, log onto the Social Security website, and talk to a financial planner if you can.

If you've put it off for years, congratulations for taking this step. I know it was very tedious – gathering the information from so many different places and putting it all on paper. With any luck (and good planning), your final figures give you the picture you were hoping for – that you're on track for a comfortable retirement – maybe even sooner than you thought.

If you have more questions about retirement, please take the opportunity to visit my website, RetiredLivingToday.com and check out some of my articles on the retirement lifestyle. You may gain some insight on topics like Medicare and insurance, security for your home, why you should set up a living trust for you and your spouse, and even how to deal with aging parents and the decisions you must make.

I have several books planned to follow this one. Check back on my website. I'll be announcing each new book there. You can also go to my Author Page on Amazon to see all my books:

amazon.com/Dianne-Terry/e/B07L6M16D8

Congratulations! You're on your way to retirement – the retirement of your dreams.

Please review my book

As an independent author, my book lives or dies by the reviews it receives. Please go over to the marketplace where you bought this book and leave an honest review to help others decide if this book is right for them.

Thank you!!

Author Page

Dianne Terry has been writing most of her life. She began writing fiction in grade school – short stories and poetry. But she began her non-fiction career several years ago – writing articles for magazines and starting a blog.

She was first published in *Good Ole Days* magazine in 2013 and won a city-wide writing contest in Kansas City in 2014.

In 2017 she started her first blog – about retirement. She has written many articles for her blog, covering the planning that needs to take place before retirement and how best to do that. She also writes about those life issues one faces with aging parents. The topics are varied but all involve life as a retiree.

Now that she has been retired two years, she is even more positive that helping people plan for retirement is her "calling."

Over 50% of Americans getting close to retirement indicate they are very concerned about being able to afford to retire. Her mission is help people, one at a time, plan for retirement.

So, what does retirement look like for Dianne and her husband? Over the past two years, they have taken a couple of cruises, spent time at their lake home in northern Arkansas, visited friends and family, and played golf, lots of golf.

When they aren't travelling or playing golf, Dianne and her husband spend their time in the Kansas City area, cheering on the Chiefs and Royals and staying active in their church.

She loves writing articles for her two blogs, Retired Living Today.com (about retirement) and now ChosenandLovedbyHim.com (a Christian blog), reading and writing books.

More Books and Resources from the Author

All of these books can be found on the Author's Page on Amazon using this link:

https://www.amazon.com/Dianne-Terry/e/B07L6M16D8

or go to Amazon.com and type in Dianne Terry in the search bar.

eBooks

Do You Know What It Takes? Planning for Your Best Retirement

Paperbacks

Do You Know What It Takes? Planning for Your Best Retirement

Journals
My Bible Study Journal
My Pocket Prayer List Journal
Pocket Prayer List v2
Pocket Prayer List v3
My Prayer Journal
Our Family's Heritage Through Recipes
Today, I Choose Gratitude
My Cancer Journey: Kicking Cancer's Butt!!

My Cancer Journey: Kick Cancer Live Free
The Family Medical Journal 8 x 10 size
The Family Medical Journal 6 x 9 size
Beat Cancer Journal
Kick Cancer's Butt!
Gratitude Journal

Coloring Books
Mandala Coloring Book

Gift Books
Sisters
Puppy Love

Appendix A: Retirement Income Workbook

Guaranteed Income

Social Security

Your Annual Expected Income $ _____

Your Spouse's Annual Expected Income $ _____

Subtotal Social Security $ _____

Pension Plans

Your Annual Expected Income Pension 1 $ _____

Your Spouse's Annual Expected Income $ _____

Additional _____ $ _____

Additional _____ $ _____

Additional _____ $ _____

Subtotal Pension Plans $ _____

Annuities

Expected Annual Income Annuity 1 $ _____

Expected Annual Income Annuity 2 $ _____

Additional _____ $ _____

Additional _____ $ _____

Subtotal Annuities $ _____

Net Rental Income

Expected Annual Amount $ _____

Additional _____ $ _____

Additional _____ $ _____

Subtotal Rent $ _____

Total Guaranteed Income $ _____

Assets

Bank Accounts

Annual Expected Income Account 1 $ _____

Additional Accounts _____ $ _____

Additional Accounts _____ $ _____

Additional Accounts _____ $ _____

Additional Accounts _____ $ _____

Subtotal Annual Bank Account Income $ _____

Certificates of Deposit (CDs)

Annual Expected Income Account 1 $ _____

Additional Accounts _____ $ _____

Additional Accounts _____ $ _____

Additional Accounts _____ $ _____

Additional Accounts _____ $ _____

Subtotal Annual CD Income $ _____

Your Home

Your Home's Current Value $ _____

Home Equity Loan Amount $ _____

Expected Equity Loan Income per year $ _____

Reverse Mortgage Income per year $ _____

Subtotal Annual Income from Home $ _____

Subtotal Assets Page 2 $ _____

Assets (cont'd)

Qualified Plans

401(k)

Account from _____ $ _____

Account from _____ $ _____

Account from _____ $ _____

Account from _____ $ _____

Account from _____ $ _____

Subtotal 401(k) Annual Income $ _____

403(b)

Account from _____ $ _____

Account from _____ $ _____

Account from _____ $ _____

Subtotal 403(b) Annual Income $ _____

457

Account from _____ $ _____

Account from _____ $ _____

Account from _____ $ _____

Subtotal 457 Annual Income $ _____

Solo 401(k)

Account from _____ $ _____

Account from _____ $ _____

Account from _____ $ _____

Subtotal Solo 401(k) Annual Income $ _____

Subtotal Assets Page 3 $ _____

Assets (cont'd)

Miscellaneous Plans

IRA

Account from _____ $ _____

Account from _____ $ _____

Account from _____ $ _____

Account from _____ $ _____

Account from _____ $ _____

Subtotal IRA Annual Income $ _____

SEP IRA

Account from _____ $ _____

Account from _____ $ _____

Account from _____ $ _____

Subtotal SEP IRA Annual Income $ _____

Simple IRA

Account from _____ $ _____

Account from _____ $ _____

Account from _____ $ _____

Subtotal Simple IRA Annual Income $ _____

Roth IRA

Account from _____

Account from _____ $ _____

Account from _____ $ _____

Subtotal Roth IRA Annual Income $ _____

Subtotal Assets Page 4 $ _____

Assets (cont'd)

Miscellaneous Plans (cont'd)

Whole Life Insurance With Cash Value

Account from _____ $ _____

Account from _____ $ _____

Account from _____ $ _____

Account from _____ $ _____

Account from _____ $ _____

Subtotal Whole Life Annual Income $ _____

Additional Misc. Sources of Income

Account from _____ $ _____

Account from _____ $ _____

Account from _____ $ _____

Subtotal Misc. Sources Annual Income $ _____

Subtotal Assets Page 5 $ _____

Subtotal Assets Page 2 $ _____

Subtotal Assets Page 3 $ _____

Subtotal Assets Page 4 $ _____

Total Spendable Assets $ _____

Calculations

1. Guaranteed Income

Total Guaranteed Assets from Page 1 $ _____

2. Assets

Total Spendable Assets from page 5 $ _____

Subtract a cash cushion from Spendable
Assets. This should be 1—2 years worth of
expenses not covered by guaranteed income. $ _____

Net Spendable Assets $ _____

Multiply the Net Spendable Assets
by your risk tolerance —
    0.03 Very conservative
    0.04 Traditional
    0.05 Ok with some risk but can cut back
        If the market turns for the worse.

Initial Annual Spendable Assets $ _____

3. Calculate Total Annual Income

Add Total Guaranteed Income #1
to Initial Annual Spendable Assets #2 $ _____

Total Annual Income $ _____

4. Calculate Total Monthly Income

Divide Total Annual Income by 12 $ _____

Congratulations! You Did It!

www.ingramcontent.com/pod-product-compliance
Lightning Source LLC
Chambersburg PA
CBHW070943210326
41520CB00021B/7034